TONGUELESS

Rojbîn Arjen Yiğit

Out-Spoken Press
London

Published by Out-Spoken Press,
PO Box 78744
London, N11 9FG

All rights reserved
© Rojbîn Arjen Yiğit

The rights of Rojbîn Arjen Yiğit to be identified as the author of this work have been asserted by them in accordance with section 77 of the Copyright, Designs and Patents Act 1988.

A CIP record for this title is available from the British Library.

This book is in copyright. Subject to statutory exception and to provisions of relevant collective licensing agreements, no reproduction of any part may take place without the written permission of Out-Spoken Press.

First edition published 2024
ISBN: 9781738412556

Typeset in Futura and Adobe Caslon
Design by Patricia Ferguson
Printed and bound by Print Resources

Out-Spoken Press is supported using public funding by the National Lottery through Arts Council England.

TONGUELESS

CONTENTS

VIOLENT PASSAGE	1
LONGING	2
MURMUR OF	3
MY CONSTANT WALK	5
IN AUGUST	6
DWELLINGS	7
ABNORMAL FABRICATIONS	8
I DID NOT DISRESPECT ANY SPRING	9
POST (ANAPHYLAXIS)	10
PEARL YOUR DARLINGS	11
DOUBLES	12
ŞITLA RIHANÊ / BASIL SEEDLING	13
YOU ARE A TAR PIT	14
EXIT	15
DAUGHTERLAND	17
MALA TE AVA / MAY YOUR HOME BE BUILT	18
ACKNOWLEDGEMENTS	21

for dayê & bavo, for creating all of my tongues

VIOLENT PASSAGE

Leak the river from me my father's first place of swim the fish and pistachios handfuls mouthfuls mourning a soil. Look, the black roses. Look, the hands of the picker. The son returned. Look, the mother. Folded in half in the living room, look she bleeds. She too, bleeds. We too pray to the war drum. Our weddings, each a bursting noose against our necks. My sisters stand to şevko. Here are the colours we love. Seven and spiteful I spat at my mother tongue. Cut her jugular and let it steady out of me, today she is a handful of soil under my pillow. In every dream I beg her for a metaphor, for even a nightmare. My father's fist is in the wall and mother screams into its mouth. Death anniversaries I count on my fingers, the first year then the tenth then the, look. We too die. Look, here is our funeral.

LONGING

in grass I wake with guts spilling
rain-dappled arms elbows soiled
ingrained a green tinge I don't want to
write anymore each word dissects me
out of myself each word a hinge in my gums
hook grabbing my ankles I want to lie to myself
and on the grass in the sun I want to become
a slow animal the barking dog scares me
I feel as though I should leave my seat
I don't know where I'm going
no one to meet I keep seeing children
keep seeing better things here I feel senseless
I can't bare the weight of myself
my whole body collapses onto me
laid out and down there's a scalpel
on my skin I've quietly started moisturising
my elbows I still hate my body
this country I keep counting the pomegranate
seeds and insist on living time is grass blade
pointed at the mornings no one knows
what comes look here look at how many
women there are each with a life laid out.

MURMUR OF

Mother's face
was a crescent
her braids in the photo
similar to mine I get a rash
thinking of her a silence made a girl
born with her belly burnt my mother
asks me do you remember anything
before the age of three?

I have a pain in my temples
although she doesn't tell me she loves me
my mother's shade is enough
I will never know the taste of the mushrooms
she cries talking about her palms
crawl into fists everything happening
now will be a memory

she's made mistakes
has torn her navel to keep
every portion of me
I'm weak but you cannot bend
my mother's wrist her back a curve
over the sink angles of her jaw clenched
and knuckles worn worked and exhausted

here is the labour: of hot water
and knife scratches of excavated
aubergines and peppers spread
with their red faces wide to the heat
here is my image
reflected an echo forwarded her never
there touch always a fear in my throat
a bulge in my chest

I am scared of what I will remember
I want to call her and make her listen
to the sound of my pressure cooker
ask her if this is the way

MY CONSTANT WALK

The steady beat
all men are brothers
except my father
I don't need to say love me
you know it from the brink
of my curls and the hair I'm
afraid to cut I want a closeness
in habits peaches in spring
persimmons in winter
singular and piercing
I want to go back to Istanbul
sit wide to hang myself out
towards the low sea
watch the greedy contraction of waves
pleating in masses of swells
I want to balance an eel on my palm
the July heat penetrating a dew
into muscles unlatching
to loosen their fascia
to tell my father he has
a brother in me

IN AUGUST

I was backless a throatful roar
a mussel sharpened shell browned
close to where citrus begged
six new words opening in Kurdish
blue lips scaled up towards dentists
decay excavated my borderline gums

creatures our women climbed
through windows forwarding to the dead
thumbs up heads down who killed
themselves at sleep every afternoon
we wanted a swim but River remained
no more

did you end up eating our soil or
kill your lover with land on a Thursday?
slowly did you pull at the worms did
his throat split red fishing out of spines
we saw him froth at the belly
sixty-three strokes later I arrive

DWELLINGS

I grew up eating without
Euphratic fish. I bit none
of their forty-six teeth
the black rose bragged
apart the collagen in my ears.
Exile is a knee in my mouth
preaching borderwards.
My mother tobaccos her finger
to a yellow delight. My mouth
pistachioed at my ends,
tip of common carp, itself
greenwards. To the blood
orange marked.
Centromere of our middle,
Grieves in vomits of kohl liners.
One cell thick at my waterline.
My knees split open,
the triangle of river, gleams.
Fear is so large, try stealing
my Euphrates: my diaphragm
will soilate you so hard; my
father's house keys will oscillate
between here and there

ABNORMAL FABRICATIONS

Mother can you touch me
so I know I am here
by the kitchen window
with three walnuts in my pocket
I nearly died twice both times
at the wanting of you
On some parched February day
you assassinated me again
I crush three walnuts under my pits
small cracklings the great noise
of the city outside the kitchen window
two men are fighting I am in Istanbul
three hours ahead of you sacred information
your friend is talking away just now.

You were in a really bad place
I can't imagine you in a worse place
boomerang refugee unloading the dishwasher
water sploshes off the dips in the mugs
a cigarette dangling off her lips
I remember you she is telling me to go easy
slamming the dishwasher shut with her hips
please let me have my shower
of anger near the road that turns home
a refusal to speak because
I am not her she would have been made
in your image you walk in with a bowl
of watermelon your presence shocks me
out of this…
sat in 10pm summer half-light
seventeen weeks since I found out
you kiss my head seconds before —

I DID NOT DISRESPECT ANY SPRING

First night away from Berlin felt like Gods
were throwing stones I wonder if my mother
remembers the flying from those two children
and their mother the street leading home past
the school round pebbles shooting their elbows
landing often on us sometimes on the pavement
I never told you that midnight how you asked
me about our wounds being the largest distance
quiet before the impact border zones the luring
delay of time I rolled one last drain of tea in the cup
I told you I have one that looks exactly like yours
scar blemished hot at my knee you too
thought your mother to be ruthless
remorse formed over a wound winter is blinding
light drags towards November
my mother will savage closer
to death by another year of being alive
in a place she hates that terror keeps me
at the departure gate I watch my father's
limp arms a date stone cracks between his molars
our hunger makes my ears itch I know nothing of God
except for my mother I keep a tangerine in my bag
mould it into my fingertips press the porous skin
to my lips knowing it will rot

POST (ANAPHYLAXIS)

Entering the sphere
with moan merging
from spleen this is not
the season of Adam's apples
bobbing oxygen rattling
to oscillations until a local
relief comes beating fingers

One has three phalanges raw
deeping for my cardiac sac
no sanctity nor dignity left
lick the pulse off my fig
dampness scaling two nail beds
palpitating aortas

Clean riots of blood pooling
a single spring tonight
cleaves for nostrils oxygen
hot still this night my gender
is steel green melting off
the bone

lining my mucosal gut
remembrances in theatres
the arteries rise my cilia
stand a deep bow round
of applause I am clasped.

PEARL YOUR DARLINGS

Yesterday I split my knee
open. My mouth did not utter
a wound slowly some yellow
the same night. Between
fifteen dreams you moved
like I'd written a letter about
disappearance. Some old fire
burnt into my patella.
I bellied myself up
with my mother's yoghurt.
I didn't understand your past
tense so why did you?
Light into the Arjen entered
and you became transparent
clotting at my synovial joint.
If I plait my hair into two
I want you to look at my split
no care to heal my knee.
When I can marvel at you
marvelling at my blood
it's far easier to let you pearl it.

DOUBLES

three raspberry heads
bounce on fingers hollowed
cream cashmere on my
elbow wiped up
four histological layers
soaked into one eye
licked to a shut
a mulberry bleached
not rage but a soiled
serenity I am misfolded
off my tertiary rounds
abnormal my sisterhood
makes teeth agitate
from needles swinging
sixty-three legs from comas
let me watch your height sister
glucose tongued, wide cave
on my belly a hot sisterhood
breaks my collagen lynches
matriarch lines to check
if I am alive I am so utterly
undoable, wide mouthed
legged up and cyanosed
utterly not here.

ŞITLA RIHANÊ / BASIL SEEDLING

I scorched my mother's womb for this world
now I wait for moths by the window
my favourite thing about being a little girl
was the honest promise of soil one I clung to my intention
to go back is a hot stone knuckled into my back

basils are green things mute to touch muffled
in their softness I wanted to be the most feared witch
in the village but still get my forehead blessed on Fridays
just before the final call to prayer collective punishment
has a frank taste my huge desire a vocalisation

as certain as destruction which is a hovering hand
my grandmother's forehead on the prayer mat
the soil of my land is like no other distinctive
and rare of forty-six degree heats when the sun
is merciless and God packs away from us

when the rain shuts his eyes on the city
roses appear black and folded in small numbers
today my land is partially underwater
land is language and to language is to know
a land denied
I am yet to press one dry between my palms

YOU ARE A TAR PIT

It has been a lifetime since I laid down in the shade
Of the pistachio tree covered with an afternoon of June
Long years of no sky no life no cranes now tomatoes
Rip upon sun your burnt shoulder leaning mine stark
Reminder of the encûr I cannot remember the pale taste

Wobbling down my chin I cannot imagine the tacky glory
Dialectic was my ocean she had nothing to carry only a singular
Shore washed girl I sold the land no more pistachio fields you know
My chest is shrinking no longer can you channel the world into me
What if we met in an open field I know a little girl

Who survived for me she held the groaning weight of life carried
Me like a caved walnut her skin dissolved into dew wet and heavy
Against small palms here I am now my tips shrivelled from when
The water carried me here is the hope I spat. Take it.

EXIT

I want
Four wounds in your withdrawal
White shot of infection left in your exit
Exchange for my grandmother's white headscarf
I hope every hour like a drowning woman
With only a singular place to go
That you will take to me
Death by blank bullets in your parched hair
You smell of salt and tell me about
Your father's whites of his loose exhaustion
I can frame him in you
Manner in which you take your precautions
I listen to the light of you
The murmur becomes a time mistake
Departure from the white hour
I need no revolution just
The upheaval of a mind starved
Give me the bottom of the river
The oval of your chin cuffs my shoulder blades
Sunbeam lent to me too briefly
I reek of lost insecurity but I am just a woman and
As a child my world was bleaker
You too had a blurred still of a mind bomb
And I know why you become a tongue revert
To a tongue cut
Flicker of languages
Security of speaking in dissolution
I was merely treading water
And now my hope is a going
Your bare ankles a single shot
A peace waiver

Here I am just a woman
With a clean forehead
Both my palms open

DAUGHTERLAND

The thought of you
Never leaves me
Hot possibility of pistachio trees
Mountain tops slick with snow
Colour of you
Sinks sixty-three feet down
I hum your name to myself
When the night is shallow
So far from home I am
Often where a stranger eats my name
I blitz into the oblivion where I see God
A sharpening light digs
Cleaves into my tonsils
No translator left to sound
My mother's descending
Silence
Her butchered tongue still
Even now begging for her mouth
Limp and dry on gravel
The thought of a country of mine
Hangs me
Cuts me into the shape of
A never-hope of a landless illness
I have taken years to
Drive myself far from that holy dream
But I think often of a bare field
September a raw sun on soil
Mattresses laid on rooftops
My face seeds out a hot sob.

MALA TE AVA / MAY YOUR HOME BE BUILT

Motherland is a cold sweat in my dreams
Chronic waves of hysteria
All of my actions are contemplations
Can you guess the word I am thinking of
I don't know how to translate myself
This lamp post is foreign it butters the guts out of me
Grandmother places my fingers to her temples
She has lost her sense of smell
The deq on her chest has lost its tone
I want the same one, but this is a figment
I don't even know who she is
The alarm is bright it keeps me up at night
Soon it will be too late and
I cannot stop the time
She moves the beads and prays
She cannot kneel anymore
But God knows her from her breath
Memory is a flicker against my age
The flies and slabs of cheese would
Chase me it was my grandfathers hand
His black moustache is all that remains
Please speak no longer of War
I am yet to find a shoulder for my head
To rest is the dough my mother folds twelve times
I must not pronounce a single wrongdoing
This is the holy rolling
I do not know the foreigners love
But I can wish for your home to be built
Language is to torment
Teach me to spell tounge

ACKNOWLEDGEMENTS

Many thanks to the editors of the following places where some poems from this pamphlet first appeared: *Prototype*, Issue 5 and the collaborative poetry anthology for Association of Anaesthetists.

Rojbîn Arjen Yiğit is a writer and poet. She is trilingual, her poetry probes the themes of language, exile and womanhood. Amongst other places, her work has been published in *Wasafiri*, *Prototype*, *Extra Teeth* and *Propel Magazine*. *Tongueless* is her debut poetry pamphlet.

SELECTED OTHER TITLES BY OUT-SPOKEN PRESS

Down • Rebecca McCutcheon
Bark, Archive Splinter • Jay Gao
Boiled Owls • Azad Ashim Sharma
[...] • Fady Joudah
Vulgar Errors / Feral Subjects • Fran Lock
State of Play: Poets of East & Southeast Asian Heritage in Conversation • Eds. Eddie Tay & Jennifer Wong
Nude as Retrospect • Alex Marlow
Today Hamlet • Natalie Shapero
G&T • Oakley Flanagan
sad thing angry • Emma Jeremy
Trust Fall • William Gee
Cane, Corn & Gully • Safiya Kamaria Kinshasa
apricot • Katie O'Pray
Mother of Flip-Flops • Mukahang Limbu
Dog Woman • Helen Quah
Caviar • Sarah Fletcher
Somewhere Something is Burning • Alice Frecknall
flinch & air • Laura Jane Lee
Fetch Your Mother's Heart • lisa luxx
Seder • Adam Kammerling
54 Questions for the Man Who Sold a Shotgun to My Father • Joe Carrick-Varty
Lasagne • Wayne Holloway-Smith
Mutton Rolls • Arji Manuelpillai
Contains Mild Peril • Fran Lock
Epiphaneia • Richard Georges
Stage Invasion: Poetry & the Spoken Word Renaissance • Pete Bearder
The Neighbourhood • Hannah Lowe
The Games • Harry Josephine Giles
Songs My Enemy Taught Me • Joelle Taylor